Solving Cold Cases Vol. 8

True Crime Stories That Took Years to Crack

Andrew J. Clark

Warning
Throughout the book, there are some descriptions of murders and crime scenes that some people might find disturbing. There might be also some language used by people involved in the murders that may not be appropriate.

Note
Words in italic are quoted words from verbatim and have been reproduced as is, including any grammatical errors and misspelled words.

ISBN 9798720959708

Printed in the United States

Contents

Warming up Cold Cases

Murder, mayhem, and wanton destruction. They are the kind of stories you hear about on the six o'clock news. Tales of horrific violence that leave people dead and families forever shattered. But as heinous as these crimes are, we can count ourselves lucky that most of the perpetrators soon end up behind bars. Some cases, however, continue to elude investigators. Leads that were once promising have long gone cold. These are the cases that come to haunt homicide detectives, keeping them up at night wondering why no clues are forthcoming.

Just take the heartbreaking case of Tina Faelz. She was a 14-year-old girl who had just begun her freshman year of high school. She didn't fit in well with her peers and was bullied so badly that she refused to wait at her neighborhood bus stop and started walking to school instead. It was during one of these walks that she was horrifically murdered, stabbed multiple times, and left to bleed to death. Her killing would haunt her community and most especially her classmates forever.

Even those who had picked on this poor girl were deeply traumatized by her death. Yet police could not find a lead in this case. It seemed like someone had just ambushed the girl out of the blue and then disappeared into thin air. But once this cold case was finally solved decades later, the killer's identity would shock everyone. It was not some random stranger after all, but someone who had been right there in their midst all along.

Once cold cases like this are solved, the results are often quite surprising. And this book is full of cases just like this. Because just under the surface of many cold cases are mind-blowing details that only come to the surface when the cold case finally begins to warm up.

Carla Jan Walker
Justice at Long Last

Who: Carla Jan Walker
Where: Fort Worth, Texas
When: February 1974
Suspects: Glen Samuel McCurley
Conviction: Pending

Background Information

Carla Walker was a popular high school girl—a cheerleader—who dated the school's star football player, Rodney McCoy. She dearly loved her boyfriend, who had just given her a "promise ring" for Valentine's Day. But two days later, on the evening of February 16, 1974, the lives of these two young lovers would be tragically disrupted.

On February 16, 1974, Carla Walker and her boyfriend Rodney McCoy were having an enjoyable Saturday evening in Fort Worth, Texas. Their school was hosting a dance party in honor of the recent Valentine's Day, and after stopping for a bite at a local eatery, they went to check it out. Carla looked beautiful and stunning in a blue dress, and Rodney was seen sporting both a dashing suit and a big grin. After the dance, Rodney took his date to the local bowling alley, Brunswick Ridglea Bowl. But when the couple began to make out in the parking lot, a jealous observer decided to run diabolical interference on this football star.

As the couple kissed inside Rodney's car, Carla was positioned with her back to the passenger door. The door wasn't locked, and the couple was so preoccupied with their heavy petting session that they didn't notice a stranger approaching from that direction. When the man yanked open the door, Carla fell right out of the vehicle. Before he could even reach out to grab his girlfriend, Rodney was struck several times across the head with the handle of a handgun their assailant was wielding. He tried to fight back, but blood flowing from a gash over his eyes made it hard for him to even see. Fading in and out of consciousness, he heard Carla shouting, "I'll go with you, just don't shoot him!" and then, from farther away, "Go get my dad!" In his injured daze, Rodney didn't see the assailant and Carla leave, and by the time he revived himself enough to get out of the car and look for her, she was long gone.

The Investigation

As soon as he had enough strength to get behind the wheel, Rodney McCoy peeled out of the parking lot of the bowling alley and headed for Carla's house. Carla's mom, Charlene, answered the door to find a battered and bruised Rodney trembling outside. The Walkers whisked him into their home and summoned medical help while he told his horrific story.
Mr. Walker, upon learning that something terrible had happened to his daughter, took off to the Brunswick Ridglea Bowl. He found it already closed, however, without a car in sight. After fruitlessly "pounding on the door, he didn't know what else to do but go home.

By this time the police had arrived, and Rodney was able to give them a surprisingly detailed description of the assailant. He described him as a "clean-cut, slender young man of about 20, with short-cropped, wavy hair, who talked with a Texas drawl and stood about 5 feet, 11 inches, wearing a shiny green sleeveless vest and a near-white cowboy hat."

A manhunt for Carla and her kidnapper was launched immediately. This search consisted of "foot, horseback, car, and helicopter" patrols covering a wide area. Just a couple of days later, Fort Worth authorities were notified that a young woman's body had been discovered in the vicinity of Benbrook Lake. The corpse was only partially clad and it was obvious that she had been sexually assaulted and tortured.

Carla's parents were given the grim task of identifying the body and confirmed that it was indeed their daughter. A subsequent autopsy indicated that she had been strangled about two and a half days before the discovery of her body. Toxicology results showed that she had been injected with morphine and other chemicals, apparently to sedate her while she was being held against her will. As you might imagine, this news was a terrible blow to Carla's loved ones. Her poor mother screamed inconsolably, and her boyfriend Rodney literally passed out in shock.

For what was to become a cold case, the strange thing about Carla's murder is that not just one but several suspects soon came out of the woodwork. Even more bizarrely, more than one person actually came forward to *confess* to the killing.

First, of course, police looked into Carla's boyfriend Rodney McCoy. Becoming a suspect after being attacked and having his girlfriend literally ripped from his arms certainly didn't ease Rodney's pain. But since significant others so often are the perpetrators, the police would have been remiss not to at least look into the possibilities. After it was discovered that Carla had been held for several days after the attack, however, Rodney was off the hook. He had spent those days recovering from his own injuries and telling police everything he could remember about the assault.

Another man who popped up on police radar was a local car thief named Glen McCurley. What caused investigators to connect him to Carla's case was the fact that he had previously purchased a .22 Ruger pistol—and they had found a magazine from the same weapon in the bowling alley parking lot the night Carla was taken. However, McCurley explained that his gun had been stolen during a fishing trip and he hadn't reported the theft because his criminal record made him hesitant to contact police. Without any other evidence linking him to the crime, investigators pushed McCurley to the back burner as they continued to search for additional suspects.

They seemed to get a big break when 21-year-old Fort Worth resident Tommy Ray Kneeland claimed to be Carla's killer. Since Kneeland was already being tried for two other killings at the time, police were perfectly willing to believe him. Just to be thorough, though, they gave him a lie detector test relating to

Carla's kidnapping and murder—and he failed. It boggles the mind why someone would confess to felonies he didn't commit, but Kneeland, who was likely already headed for life in prison for his other crimes, may have just enjoyed playing mind games with the police.

The Carla Walker case had already cooled off considerably by 1977 when one Jimmy Dean Sasser came forward and claimed that he was the guilty party. Authorities obligingly charged him with kidnapping and murder and sent him to jail to await trial. But several months later, Sasser recanted his confession, claiming that he'd simply made it "because his marriage had fallen apart and he was depressed." With no other evidence against him, authorities were forced to take him at his word and release him.

Then over 40 years passed before another breakthrough—a real one, this time—finally emerged in September of 2020. It was then that DNA extracted from Carla's clothing all those years ago was taken to Othram, a private lab that specializes in modern DNA identification techniques. Othram technicians created a DNA profile from the decades-old samples, and it established a familial link between three brothers whose last name was McCurley.

This, of course, brought Glen McCurley onto the center stage once again. Investigators then produced a smoking gun by taking some garbage from a trashcan in front of McCurley's house and extracting therefrom a DNA sample from McCurley himself. This sample proved to be an exact match for the DNA that had been found on Carla's clothing, and this allowed the cops to get an arrest warrant for the man.

When they brought him into custody, McCurley told them a decidedly different story than the one he'd concocted some 45 years ago. Unable to explain away the DNA evidence, he tried to portray himself as some kind of misguided hero. He admitted to taking Carla but claimed that he had been trying to save her. He said he was leaving the bowling alley when he saw Rodney beating her. McCurley rushed over and separated the two, and in his telling, Carla was glad to escape to the safety of his own vehicle—and very, very grateful for his protection. She hugged

him, and the two began to kiss… and then things got out of control, and the next thing he knew she was dead.
But since it's kind of hard to accidentally rape, beat, strangle, and inject someone with morphine, detectives weren't exactly lining up to buy this completely absurd cockamamie story. 77-year-old Glen McCurley was arrested on September 21, 2020, and officially charged with Carla Walker's murder.

The Conviction

As of this writing, Glen McCurley is still being held at Tarrant County Jail in Houston, Texas, with his bail set for $100,000. Having threatened to do himself in, he is under close observation. Authorities say that he has since given a full confession, and so, while his trial has not yet taken place, a conviction is looking pretty likely.

His former neighbors are fairly shocked. McCurley, a married man with two kids, had been a model member of the neighborhood. Despite his previous convictions for car theft, he had apparently evolved into a churchgoing pillar of the community. As one former neighbor who does not wish to be identified put it, "I just absolutely cannot believe it. He was a quiet man; they were a very nice family. They were active in church; he was always in church. It's unbelievable. I would never have guessed."

But as they say, you shouldn't judge a book by its cover, and even those who seem to be good people could turn out to be killers in the end.

How DNA Nabbed Sarah Yarborough's Killer

Who: Sarah Yarborough
Where: Federal Way, Washington
When: December 1991
Suspects: Patrick Leon Nicholas
Conviction: Pending

Background Information

Sarah Yarborough was a happy 16-year-old girl. She was a good student who regularly made the honor roll at Federal Way High School, and she had big plans for the future. Sadly, she would not be able to implement them after falling victim to a brutal killer on December 14, 1991.

On the day she disappeared, Sarah drove herself to school so that she could board a bus to go to a school dance competition. Her car was later found parked at the school, but there was no sign of Sarah herself. As the other students boarded the bus, she was "noticeably missing from the team." A short time later, her corpse was found in a wooded area by the school tennis court.

The two 12-year-old boys who happened upon the corpse also seemed to have happened upon the killer. It was around nine in the morning that the kids noticed a guy stepping out of the woods. The sight seemed odd to them, so they waited for the man to depart and then went into the woods he had just left. There they found Sarah's dead body, still sporting her school uniform. She had been brutally raped before she had the life choked out of her.

The Investigation

The police were called immediately and a major search for
Sarah's killer got underway. The story dominated the local news,
and the community at large was very much involved in the efforts
to solve the tragic murder. Many residents supplied anecdotal
information, but nothing proved substantial enough to produce
any major leads.

There was a basic physical description of the assailant thanks to
the boys who had seen him leaving the wooded area where they
found Sarah's body. They said he was in his late teens to early
20s, with shaggy, sandy-colored hair and blue eyes. A police
artist duly produced a forensic sketch, but nobody recognized the
man it depicted.

However, the perpetrator himself had left some telltale evidence
behind at the crime scene. He had deposited semen on Sarah's
clothes, and this was collected and cross-referenced with a DNA
database. DNA forensics was quite new in the early 1990s,
however, and initially, it did not produce any results. As evidence
in an unsolved homicide, the DNA samples were stored away as
the years continued to go by and the case became colder and
colder.

It wasn't until 2018, when detectives began to scour through
genealogy databases to which citizens have voluntarily submitted
DNA samples, that they were able to find not just suspects but
people who were related to suspects. Then, using a method
called genetic genealogy, they were able to backtrack through a
family tree and narrow down the personal family of the suspect.
By the fall of 2019, they were able to whittle their pool of relatives
down to just two brothers.

The brothers were both convicted rapists. Judging from their
criminal history alone, either one could have been the culprit in
the Sarah Yarborough case. But one of the brothers had already
submitted a DNA sample for a previous offense, and it proved
that he lwas innocent of this one. That could only mean that the
DNA from the semen found on Sarah belonged to his brother,
and this is what led the police to Patrick Nicholas.

Nicholas had served time in prison for rape in 1983. He was 55 years old in 2019 and would have been 27 years old at the time of Sarah's murder—a little older than what the two young witnesses had guessed, but not by much.

Now, all investigators had to do to establish a more direct link was to collect a fresh DNA sample from Nicholas and confirm that he was a match. They would need a warrant to compel him to give them such a sample, but any discarded item on which he had inadvertently left his DNA, such as a paper cup or a half-eaten meal, was fair game. As it happened, Nicholas was a smoker, so when he dropped a cigarette butt, detectives collected and sent it to the lab to be tested. Sure enough, it came back as a match. This was all the police needed to bring Nicholas into custody.

The Conviction

Patrick Nicholas was charged with first-degree murder in October of 2019. He has since pled not guilty and is still awaiting trial as of this writing.

Cynthia Miller
Did They Finally Find Her Killer?

Who: Cynthia Miller
Where: West Virginia
When: August 1981
Suspects: Earl James Robbins
Conviction: Pending

Background Information

Cynthia Miller was a 27-year-old school teacher in rural West
Virginia. She was soon to transfer to a better-paying job at Park
Junior High School, and she was looking forward to it. She was
also engaged to a local police officer named Gary O'Neal.
Cynthia and Gary already lived together in a modest home which
they shared with a tenant who rented out the first floor.

The night before the wedding, Gary O'Neal went to visit his
parents. Cynthia Miller was gunned down shortly after his
departure. Gary telephoned Cynthia several times after he left,
but she was already dead. Wondering why his fiancée wouldn't
pick up the phone, he cut short his visit with his parents and
headed back to the home he shared with Cynthia. Even Gary's
experience as a policeman hadn't prepared him for what he
found when he got there. As soon as he stepped through the
door, he saw the bullet-riddled body of his bride-to-be. She had
been shot several times at close range.

The Investigation

Bloody as it was, the crime scene was also very unusual in a
number of ways. Cynthia had been shot almost execution-style,
yet there was no indication of a break-in and no indication of any
other disturbance in the home. Nothing had been stolen, and
there was no indication of sexual assault.

To investigators, this seemed like either a crime of revenge or passion. The fact that the victim's intended husband was a police officer might easily explain a revenge motive—perhaps a criminal whom Gary had arrested had decided to get back at him by hurting his bride. But much as they wanted to, they couldn't rule out a crime of passion. What if Gary and Cynthia had argued, and he had snapped and started shooting?

Gary's fellow officers were hesitant to even consider this angle; he was a respected colleague and, by all accounts, a loving boyfriend. But standard police procedure is to treat a murder victim's loved ones as potential suspects in just about any case. So they went ahead and interviewed several of Cynthia's family members and friends—yet they couldn't find anyone with any real motive for murdering her. As for Gary, it helped that he had tried to call Cynthia several times. Phone records backed this fact up, and they also indicated that Gary was away from the house when Cynthia was killed.

Mostly, though, there was just no conceivable reason for him to kill her. As a detective who worked on this case—Morgan Bragg—put it, "From what the original investigators put together in the file, it appears there weren't any signs of any kind of discord that particular night. We haven't uncovered anything that makes us think they were having any kind of turmoil the night before their wedding." There was no big fight, and no last-minute calling off of wedding plans. In other words, there was no reason for Gary to hurt his fiancée.

Gary himself always maintained that he had no idea who killed Cynthia—and he maintained this until the day he died. Yes, sadly enough, Gary passed away before this long-cold case was eventually solved.

In 2017, new eyes began to look at Cynthia Miller's murder and found a connection with a former local resident named Earl James Robbins. As of this writing, scant details about how Robbins was connected to this cold case have been released. It is known, however, that he has a long criminal record and prior convictions for kidnapping and rape. In fact, he was already in prison for a rape he had committed in 2005 when police made the connection between him and Cynthia's death.

If Robbins is indeed her killer, with his track record of sexual deviance, it wouldn't be hard to imagine that sexual predation was his motive. Of course, the initial investigation ruled that out, because Cynthia was not sexually assaulted.

Could it be that something startled Robbins before he could rape her so that instead he simply shot her and fled the scene? Did someone come to the door perhaps? Or pull into the driveway? As of right now, there are still more questions than answers, and Earl James Robbins isn't providing any—he has pled not guilty.

The Conviction

As of this writing, Earl James Robbins is still awaiting trial.

Rayna Rison
Did Her Boyfriend Do It?

Who: Rayna Rison
Where: La Porte, Indiana
When: March 1993
Suspects: Jason Tibbs
Conviction: 2014

Background Information

Rayna Rison, the daughter of Ben and Karen Rison, came into this world on May 6, 1976. She grew up in the small-town environment of La Porte, Indiana. She attended La Porte High School, where she was an honor student and also performed in the school band, mastering three different musical instruments. By her sophomore year, she was working part-time at La Porte's animal hospital. Rayna loved animals and hoped to become a veterinarian one day.

Everything was going fine—except for one thing. Rayna had recently broken up with a boyfriend, Jason Tibbs, who had become obsessed with her. She had called off the relationship and moved on, but her ex-boyfriend had refused to do so. And when jealous Jason heard that Rayna was planning to go on a date with a boy named Matt Elser after she got off work on the evening of March 26, 1993, he apparently decided to intervene.

Rayna Rison's shift at the Pine Lake Animal Hospital was scheduled to run from 4:00 to 6:00 PM that day. After that, she was supposed to meet up with her high school classmate Matt Elser. Rayna had driven herself to work, but Matt was going to pick her up there and take her on their date in his own vehicle. He showed up on schedule, but neither Rayna nor her car was there, and the animal hospital was already closed for the evening.

Unsure what else to do, Matt got back in his car and circled around the block a bit before heading to Rayna's home. He knocked on the door, hoping to find Rayna inside, but it was her father Ben who answered. Ben, becoming just as worried as Matt, informed the young man that he hadn't heard from Rayna either. Rayna's parents waited a few more hours before heading to the police station to declare that their daughter was missing.

The Investigation

The police informed Rayna's family that it would be another 24 hours before they would be able to file an official missing person report, so they began to search the town on their own. They called up everyone they knew, asking if anyone had seen or heard anything about Rayna. In the following days, they also plastered every corner of the town with fliers featuring a picture of Rayna.

These efforts finally paid off when a few people came forward claiming to have seen Rayna speaking with two young guys outside the animal hospital on the night of her disappearance. According to these eyewitnesses, the discussion seemed to be a heated one, and Rayna appeared to be arguing with one of the young men in particular. Dramatic as this was, the bystanders assumed it was some kind of teenage love triangle gone bad and hadn't thought too much more about it until they saw the fliers.

Hearing this, police began to wonder whether Matt hadn't been telling the whole truth about what happened that evening. But when they interviewed him again, he stuck to the story about how he arrived at the animal hospital to find Rayna nowhere in sight, and when they checked his story with Rayna's parents, it seemed to check out.

The next day, Rayna's car was discovered on the side of a lonesome stretch of the country road some nine miles away from the animal hospital. The vehicle's hood was up as if the driver had experienced some kind of mechanical problem. However, the keys were still in the ignition, and when the policeman on the scene tried to start the car for himself, the engine fired to life without hesitation. There was apparently nothing wrong with this vehicle, which made investigators think that perhaps this car had been staged to look like it was in distress. But why? And by whom?

Rayna's purse was still in the vehicle, and so was a ring. When that ring was identified as belonging to her ex-boyfriend Jason Tibbs, the police naturally had some questions for the young man. However, Tibbs explained it away by saying that he had previously done some car repairs for Rayna, and having taken off the ring while he was doing the work, had simply forgotten to retrieve it.

Be that as it may, investigators still wanted to know what Tibbs had been up to on the day Rayna vanished. Tibbs claimed to have an alibi; he insisted that he'd been out with his friends playing a goofy game they called "fox hunting"—which apparently had nothing at all to do with foxes. These small-town youngsters would play an elaborate game of hide-and-seek in cars outfitted with CBs, giving little bits and pieces of information about their location so that the "fox hunter" could try to find them. When the cops questioned Tibbs's buddies, they admitted that they had indeed been fox hunting day. However, none of them could confirm that Tibbs was actually among them.

As the days turned into weeks, Rayna's case received national attention when it was featured on the true-crime program *America's Most Wanted*. This turned up a tip that police should head out to a local thoroughfare called Fall Road, some seven miles from Rayna's abandoned vehicle. When they got there, they found a letterman jacket that belonged to Matt Elser. This led to some more finger-pointing back at Matt, who had to then explain why his jacket was there, but it ultimately didn't help the investigation very much.

Then, on April 26, 1993, a local guy was fishing with his young daughter when they made a grisly discovery. A dead body had washed up on the other side of the pond where they were fishing. Investigators swarmed into the area and found a "fully-clothed body with two logs across its back." The body was soon confirmed to be Rayna's, and (as if the logs on her back weren't a clear enough giveaway) an autopsy established the cause of death as murder.

Following the sad discovery of Rayna's corpse, investigators received a new lead when they were tipped off by a local that Rayna's own brother-in-law, Ray McCarty, could be a suspect.

McCarty was married to Rayna's sister Lori, but he had made sexual advances on Rayna in the past. In fact, he had gotten Rayna pregnant when she was only 13 years old. This resulted in him being arrested for child molestation and Rayna getting an abortion. He was given a three-year sentence but was let out on parole in January of 1993—shortly before Rayna was killed. Had McCarty taken out some kind of warped vengeance on Rayna? It seemed possible, but without any concrete evidence, the case fizzled out and went cold.

It was nearly two years before police got what could be called, at best, a false lead. When they stopped the van of one Larry Hall, who was wanted on an attempted kidnapping charge, they found that he had newspaper clippings about Rayna in his vehicle and seemed obsessed with her case. Not only that, he actually admitted that he was the one who had killed her. The cops, however, soon figured out that Hall had been in Kentucky when Rayna was killed, making it impossible for him to be the murderer. He was, however, *a* murderer—he had killed a 15-year-old girl named Jessica Roach—and he apparently figured that since his days were numbered anyway, he might as well have a little fun playing mind games with the police.

After backing out of this cruel dead-end, investigators resumed their search for other leads, and in 1998 they refocused their attention on Rayna's brother-in-law, Ray McCarty. They managed to obtain a search warrant, and when they took a look around his property, it was his car that seemed most incriminating. They discovered several handguns, a stun gun, and bloodstains.

Shocking, of course, and suspicious, sure—but none of that should have exempted them from doing basic police work such as determining whose blood it was and whether McCarty had even owned this car at the time of Rayna's death five years before. But instead of bothering with that, they simply rushed off to file charges—and had their case thrown out of court when it turned out that McCarty was an avid hunter and the blood belonged to one of the many woodland creatures he had slaughtered over the years. They probably could have gotten him on a poaching charge, but this writer's bet is that they were too embarrassed to try.

It was another decade before a new break in the case emerged. In March of 2008, a guy named Ricky Hammons came forward and claimed that he had important details about what had happened to Rayna. Now, Hammons happened to be in prison for murder himself, and as indicated by Larry Hall's false confession, the testimony of murderers must be taken with a sizable grain of salt. Not having much else to go on, though, investigators were willing to hear what Hammons had to say.

Hammons claimed that he had seen Jason Tibbs and another young man named Eric Freeman drive into his family barn in his (Hammons) sister's car. Freeman was dating Hammons' sister at the time, and she allowed him to drive her car, so this was nothing out of the ordinary. But when Hammons saw Tibbs and Freeman open the trunk, he was in for a surprise. Inside was the body of a young girl wrapped up in a blanket. Even though her body was covered, Hammons could clearly see her face—it was Rayna. The reason that Hammons gave for not coming forward at the time was a rather lame one: he "had been smoking marijuana in the barn" and was afraid that a homicide investigation would totally harsh his buzz.

Police followed up on Hammons' story by conducting an interview with Tibbs' supposed accomplice, Eric Freeman. Freeman didn't have much to say until authorities agreed to grant him immunity in 2013, but then he got a lot more loquacious. He confirmed that he was the other young man witnesses had seen at the animal hospital while Tibbs was having his heated exchange with Rayna. According to Freeman, Tibbs was trying to talk her into rekindling their relationship. His powers of persuasion failed him, however, and when Rayna refused to consider getting back together, Tibbs turned violent and punched her in the face. Then he jumped on top of her and proceeded to choke her to death, while Freeman stood idly by doing nothing at all. The bystanders who'd seen the first part of the argument apparently hadn't stuck around, so no one else intervened either.

After Tibbs strangled Rayna, Freeman helped put her lifeless corpse into the trunk of Hammons' sister's car, and they took off. Arriving at the Hammons barn, they failed to notice Ricky Hammons lurking in the shadows smoking pot. Thinking themselves unobserved, they popped the trunk, carried Rayna to the pond, and dumped her in.

Based on the testimony of both Hammons and Freeman, Tibbs himself was finally arrested for Rayna Rison's murder in August of 2013.

The Conviction

In December of 2014, Jason Tibbs was found guilty as charged and handed a sentence of 40 years. He appealed, but in the fall of 2016, the Supreme Court of Indiana rejected his efforts.

Lisa Holstead
What Really Happened?

Who: Lisa Holstead
Where: Green Bay, Wisconsin
When: August 1986
Suspects: Lou Griffin
Conviction: Pending

Background Information

Lisa Holstead was 22 years old when her life came to an abrupt end. In her 22 years, she had managed to touch the hearts of many. She was a young mother and a beloved girlfriend. Like all of us, she had her problems and difficulties from time to time— but she never could have imagined the consequences of the decision she made in reaction to one such situation.

Lisa and her boyfriend were driving back from a family gathering when they got into a heated argument. Losing her temper, she told him to stop the car, stepped out, and stormed off. He begged her to get back into the car, but Lisa wouldn't listen. She insisted that she would walk home on her own. Sadly enough, however, she never made it back.

Lisa Holstead was last seen in the early morning hours of August 12, 1986, stepping out of her boyfriend's car at the busy intersection of Mason and Taylor streets. Her boyfriend didn't want her to go, but they had been arguing, and as strong-willed, as Lisa was, there was no way he could stop her. Several witnesses saw her storm off, but this was the last that anyone saw her alive. She only lived a short distance away, but she didn't make it that far. She would disappear without a trace until her dead body surfaced in a nearby marsh.

The Investigation

There were no immediate leads to follow in the aftermath of
Lisa's murder. Since so many people had seen her leave the car,
her boyfriend wasn't a likely suspect. The best theory the cops
could come up with was that it had been a random killing—which
meant that anyone roaming the streets that night could have
been the perpetrator. Some suggested that Lisa might have
stopped at a bar along the way and accepted a ride home from a
stranger, who then turned on her and killed her. But that was just
speculation.

What was clear from the autopsy was that Lisa had been raped
and strangled to death. The murder weapon was apparently her
own blouse. She was then tossed partially nude into a marshy
area near Green Bay's Bay Port Industrial Park. Semen from her
rapist was found on her body, but while DNA testing conclusively
ruled out her boyfriend as the culprit, it couldn't be matched to
anyone else.

The case was therefore shelved until the 2010s when detectives
began to use new methods of genetic genealogy to try and solve
old cold cases. They were able to run the DNA from the semen
found on Lisa's body through genealogy databases and find
relatives of the rapist. The family tree they created led to a
Wisconsin man named Lou Griffin. Police then staged a stakeout
around Griffin's property, collecting his discarded beer cans and
cigarettes—and from the DNA he left on these, they linked him
conclusively to Lisa Holstead's death.

The Conviction

Lou Griffin, a 65-year-old resident of Racine, Wisconsin, was
arrested on October 26, 2020, on charges of intentional homicide
in the death of 22-year-old Lisa Holstead. As of this writing, he is
still waiting to stand trial.

Sherry Black
What Brought on the Attack?

Who: Sherry Black
Where: Salt Lake City, Utah
When: November 30th, 2010
Suspects: Adam Durborow
Conviction: Pending

Background Information

Sherry Black ran a bookstore called B&W Billiards and Books. This little shop was her pride and joy, and the 64-year-old could often be found behind the cash register, personally waiting on customers. That's precisely what she was doing on November 30, 2010, when tragedy struck.

When Sherry's daughter called her at work and couldn't get through, her family began to worry. Her husband Earl drove down to the store to check on her—and had the misfortune of finding Sherry lying beaten and stabbed in the back of the bookstore. She was already dead.

The Investigation

Although robbery is never really right, this scene looked a lot like a robbery gone wrong. It appeared to the police that someone had tried to rob Sherry, and instead of handing over the money, she had decided to fight back. The considerable number of defensive wounds she had showed that she had put up a pretty good fight before succumbing in the end. She had also managed to wound her attacker so severely that the crime scene was soaked in his blood—which, of course, represented a veritable treasure trove of DNA evidence. The killer also left a fingerprint and a palm print at the scene.

Detectives were understandably hopeful that this abundant physical evidence would quickly lead to a suspect. But neither the fingerprints, the palm print, nor the DNA matched anything they had on file. It did, at least, exonerate Earl. There had been some whispers that the sheer anger of the assault could be indicative of a lovers' quarrel—but it definitely wasn't Earl's blood at the scene. As Detective Joe Sutera stressed, "We've cleared all the family. We've looked at them extensively, as you have to in an investigation."

If the killer wasn't someone who knew Sherry, the only other obvious motive for the killing was a robbery. Now, the cash was still in the cash register, and tens of thousands of dollars' worth of rare, antique books were still on the shelves. But perhaps the perpetrator hadn't realized the value of the books, and perhaps he'd been too badly hurt—or too scared that the ruckus had attracted attention—to bother grabbing the cash on his way out.

So robbery was still the first thing on detectives' minds—but in this case, they were looking into a more exotic angle as well. Some time ago, Sherry had bought some valuable religious books without knowing that they were stolen. She had even sold some of the texts before the illegal book ring was broken up. Upon learning what had happened, she cooperated with authorities and helped to put away one of the dealers. Could her murder have been a revenge killing carried out by a cartel of book thieves?

Investigators couldn't say one way or the other until they unleashed some new DNA-based technology in 2017. First, they used DNA from the crime scene to create a "phenotype" sketch of the suspect by reading his genetic code to narrow down his facial features, complexion, and hair and eye color. This rendered a nice composite sketch, but the sketch wasn't what broke the case wide open. What did was the method of genetic family tree tracing already mentioned in other cases in this book.

In this technique, known as genetic genealogy, investigators use public genealogy databases to which donors have voluntarily submitted DNA to find people who are related to people who have left their DNA at crime scenes. Not the perpetrators, but their kin—sometimes even very distant kin. Even a third cousin twice removed is useful as a starting point. From here, police can trace the DNA back to more immediate family members and then eventually to the perpetrator himself.

This is how police finally found Sherry's accused killer, Adam Antonio Durborow. He apparently wasn't a book thief/assassin, just a misguided 19-year-old looking to steal some cash and not expecting his 64-year-old victim to fight back.

The Conviction

Now 29, Adam Antonio Durborow was arrested in October of 2020. As of this writing, legal proceedings against him are still ongoing.

Wendy Jerome
The Killer Close to Home

Who: Wendy Jerome
Where: Rochester, New York
When: November 1984
Suspects: Timothy Williams
Conviction: Pending

Background Information

Wendy Jerome was only 14 years old when she was cruelly taken from her family over the Thanksgiving holiday in 1984. It was supposed to be a time of happiness, love, and goodwill— yet, out there somewhere, a man with decidedly bad will pounced upon this innocent young girl.

On November 24—Thanksgiving Day—1984, young Wendy Jerome stepped out of her parents' house to walk over to a friend who lived just down the street from her. She was simply going to say hi and hand her buddy, who'd recently had a birthday, a card to commemorate the occasion.

Wendy left just before 7:00 PM. Her parents had told her not to be gone long and expected her back within an hour's time. When an hour had passed with no sign of Wendy, her family began to get nervous—and just two hours later, police showed up to inform them that their daughter had turned up dead.

The Investigation

Wendy Jerome had been ambushed by a killer on the way to her friend's house. A short time later her body was found discarded next to a dumpster behind a local school. She had been beaten to death, and her tortured remains showed evidence of a sexual assault. This tough young lady had evidently put up quite a struggle, but that only enraged her attacker, who unleashed such fury against her that what was initially a simple rape became a crime of pure hatred. Of course, only Wendy's assailant—only this murderous monster—is to blame for that. Every human being has the right to defend themselves—and the defensive wounds all over little Wendy's body showed that she did just that.

Investigators were able to collect plenty of the perpetrator's DNA from the crime scene, but back in the 1980s forensic methods of DNA identification were still in their infancy. It wasn't until the late 1990s that matching DNA with databases became routine, but initially investigators weren't able to find a match in Wendy's case. It wasn't until 2017, when the technique of familial DNA processing emerged, that a connection to the killer was finally established.

The Conviction

In September of 2020, Timothy Williams, a 56-year-old man who had lived in Rochester most of his life before moving to Florida, was arrested for Wendy's murder. Along with the DNA evidence tying him to the crime scene, Timothy had lived in close proximity to Wendy at the time of her death.

Wendy's mother, Marlene, was both surprised and elated to hear the news. She told reporters, "I never thought I would see this day, and now it's here." She only had one regret: "I just wish my husband had been alive to see this. He passed away in 2011, and I know he's up there with her, smiling and saying, 'It's over. It's finally over.'"

Or as one of the main detectives working the case, RPD Police Captain Frank Umbrino summed it up, "Marlene, I'm sorry it took so long, but we finally did it."

As of this writing, alleged killer, Timothy Williams has yet to stand trial. Although a seemingly substantial amount of evidence has piled up against him, Timothy Williams has entered an initial plea of not guilty. Stay posted for further developments.

Kimberly Ratliff
Toxic Family to Blame?

Who: Kimberly Ratliff
Where: Omaha, Nebraska
When: January 1999
Suspects: Matt Kennedy
Conviction: Pending

Background Information

Kimberly Ratliff was an ambitious and lively 22-year-old. She grew up in Montana under the care of her mom Joyce and her stepfather Les Kennedy. At the time of her death, she was employed at a factory in Omaha, Nebraska, called Airlite Plastics Co, where she was a dedicated employee who clocked in on time, without fail. Shortly after she got off her shift on January 8, 1999, however, she met with foul play.

Kimberly Ratliff was last seen leaving her place of employment at Airlite Plastics Co on January 8, 1999. It wasn't like her to run off somewhere and not tell anyone, so family and friends soon became worried about her whereabouts—and just a few days later, their worst fears would be confirmed when her dead body was discovered.

The Investigation

Police stumbled upon Kimberly Ratliff's body inside her own car in the parking lot of a local utility company called People's Natural Gas. She had apparently been savagely assaulted; she had sustained horrific injuries and parts of her body had even been mutilated. Her head had almost been severed. There wasn't very much blood in the vehicle, though, so investigators were certain that she had been killed somewhere else. This presented a major roadblock from the get-go since it meant that the majority of the evidence was at another, unknown location.

Another oddity was that Kimberly was wearing a fresh set of clothing, not what she had last been seen wearing at work. Either she had given herself a quick wardrobe change as soon as she finished her shift—or she had been dressed up by her killer. This seemingly intimate detail led police to believe that her killer was not some random stranger but instead someone who knew her.

For various reasons, the early suspicion fell upon Kimberly's non-biological relatives, the Kennedy family. Meanwhile, the Kennedys had their own suspicions as to what might have befallen their step-relative. Her stepfather, Les Kennedy, suggested that perhaps Kimberly's drug problem had gotten her into trouble with one of the drug users and dealers that she had been hanging out with. Kimberly's biological father, Jacque Ratliff, was quick to retort that it was the stress of having to live with Les Kennedy that had driven her to do drugs in the first place—but all of this was just useless innuendo that was of absolutely no help at all in figuring out who killed Kimberly.

The Conviction

In the fall of 2020, the finger of suspicion turned once more toward Kimberly's stepbrother, Matt Kennedy. He was 52 years and living in Montana when DNA evidence finally linked him to the crime. What his motive might have been remains unclear, and as of this writing, the case has not yet gone to trial.

Dilicia Mejia
A Terrible Crime

Who: Dilicia Mejia
Where: Miami, Florida
When: September 2004
Suspects: Raul Mata
Conviction: Died in custody

Background Information

Dilicia Mejia was her mother Olivia's only child, and her personal pride and joy. At the time of her daughter's death, Olivia had remarried to a man named Raul Mata, but she did not have any other children. At the age of 16, Dilicia's main concerns were her friends and her schoolwork. She studied hard and had dreams of one day becoming a police officer. She attended Miami Beach High School in Miami, Florida, and was generally well-liked by those around her. But little did she or her mother know that there was a killer right in their midst.

Olivia said goodnight to her daughter for the last time on the evening of September 16, 2004. Olivia left for her job the next morning around 5:30 AM, not knowing that Dilicia would be dead by the time she finished her shift.

The first inkling that something was wrong came when Dilicia's stepfather, Raul Mata, dialed 911 to report that he had come home to a gruesome scene. Mata happened to be a nurse, so he was no stranger to blood. But the scene he described to emergency dispatch that day was a veritable blood bath. He said that he had found his stepdaughter with her throat slit and her life had already drained out of her—and he claimed to be just as clueless as everyone else as to what might have happened to her.

The Investigation

Even so, Dilicia's stepfather was naturally a suspect in her death. Although Mata seemed to a completely upstanding character who no one could ever see committing murder, simply his close proximity to the victim required police to investigate him as part of a process of elimination. They conducted several interviews with him, and he consistently maintained his innocence. He was forthright enough to admit that his relationship with Dilicia was not the best—but he insisted that it most certainly was not bad enough that he wanted her dead. Police were not able to rule Mata out as a suspect, but they had no reason to press him further, so they moved him to the back burner for the time being.

Nevertheless, the crime scene itself seemed to suggest that the killer was *someone* who knew Dilicia. There was no forced entry, and nothing was stolen from the home. It appeared that this girl had been explicitly targeted for violence by someone who knew her.

Shortly after Dilicia's death, Olivia and Mata decided to call it quits, and Mata ended up moving clear across the country to California. He married another woman, had a child with her, and completely started over. Olivia, meanwhile, was growing more and more convinced that he had had something to do with her daughter's death.

Her suspicions were strengthened when a school counselor came forward to claim that Mata had "made improper sexual advances toward" Dilicia—and that this information was just about to be imparted to Olivia when her daughter turned up dead. Had Mata killed Dilicia to silence her? Without any further evidence linking him to the slaying, police just couldn't say for sure.

The Conviction

It wasn't until 16 years later, in 2020, that new DNA evidence surfaced that did in fact link Raul Mata to the murder of Dilicia Mejia. Police sent DNA samples recovered from underneath

Dilicia's fingernails for testing, and they came back as positive matches to Mata. This seemed to indicate that Dilicia had tried to fight Mata off, and in the process scratched some of his DNA under her nails.

Police used this evidence to arrest Raul Mata on charges of first-degree murder. That September, he was taken to Santa Cruz County Jail in California while his extradition to Florida was being processed. In October, he died from what was apparently a self-inflicted wound. Authorities say he stabbed himself in his femoral artery with an ink pen, causing a massive loss of blood.

No jury will ever get the chance to decide whether Raul Mata murdered Dilicia Mejia—but if he did, it certainly is an ironic twist of fate that he ended up bleeding to death just like Dilicia did all those years ago.

Michelle Martinko
A Life Taken Too Soon

Who: Michelle Martinko
Where: Cedar Rapids, Iowa
When: December 1979
Suspects: Jerry Lynn
Conviction: 2020

Background Information

Michelle Martinko was a happy 18-year-old girl, finishing up her senior year of high school in Cedar Rapids, Iowa before she turned up dead during the holiday season of 1979. Born on October 6, 1961, she was the youngest child of Albert and Janet Martinko—and as Janet was 44 years old at the time, Michelle was considered something of a miracle baby. As the baby of the family, raised by older parents, Michelle was showered with affection, but she certainly wasn't spoiled by it. She grew into a generous and caring young girl who always considered the feelings of others. By the time she entered Kennedy High School, she was a well-adjusted and well-liked young woman.

Michelle's only real difficulty had come when she was diagnosed with scoliosis at the age of 12. This condition required her to put on a cumbersome brace to support her back and help correct her posture, and her family later spoke of how self-conscious this made her. Fortunately, by the time she turned 14 doctors declared her condition to be corrected, and she was allowed to take off the brace. She was like a butterfly shedding her cocoon at that point, and the world took notice of the graceful young woman who emerged.

Michelle became known for her charm and good looks, especially her Farrah Fawcett style blonde hair. She was also a good student who scored high marks in her classes, and she was preparing to go off to Iowa State University after her high school graduation. Unfortunately, at the age of 18, her young life would be cut too short for these plans to come to fruition.

On the day of her disappearance, Michelle Martinko had just come back from a banquet at the Cedar Rapids Sheraton Inn which had featured a performance by her school choir. After the concert, she went to do some shopping at the Westdale Mall. It was a fairly new establishment, but Michelle had recently started a part-time job there, so she was familiar with the location and many of the other employees.

Many of those employees would later recall speaking and interacting with Michelle while she shopped that day. She was last seen in a jewelry store at around eight that evening—and at around two in the morning, her father finally broke down and called police to report that his daughter had not come home.

The Investigation

After notifying the police that his daughter was missing, Mr. Martinko himself began a frantic search, driving around town desperately looking for any sign of Michelle. Meanwhile, the police went straight to the mall, where they found Michelle's green Buick Electra parked near a JCPenney. Since the parking lot was practically deserted in the early morning hours, it was hard to miss.

When the officers approached the vehicle, their worst fears were confirmed. For inside the car, sprawled over the passenger seat, was Michelle's dead body. Closer inspection revealed that she had been stabbed multiple times in the head, throat, and upper body. Her hands also bore several slash wounds, indicating that she had tried to fend her attacker off. There was no blood outside of the car, indicating that Michelle had been killed while sitting inside. The subsequent autopsy showed that Michelle had been killed at around 8:00 PM—apparently just minutes after she was last seen shopping in the jewelry store.

Whoever had killed her seemed prepared for the task. There were no fingerprints to be found, which led forensic experts to conclude that the murderer must have worn gloves. That seemed to rule out a crime of passion, and this was not some botched robbery either; Michelle's purse, which was full of cash, had been left untouched. Nor was this a rape, as Michelle was fully clothed and showed no signs of sexual assault. It seemed that this was pure, premeditated murder. Someone had really wanted this girl dead. But who? And why?

Investigators began to pore over all of the people who knew Michelle, searching for anyone who might have had a motive to end her life. They brought several of them in for questioning, but no one seemed to provide any leads. In the meantime, local people began to gossip and spread their own theories about what might have happened to Michelle Martinko.

It was rumored that this had been a revenge killing, and while police were willing to entertain that possibility, when they got reports that Michelle had received threatening telephone calls, they could find no evidence that this had ever happened. Even more troubling was talk that another girl had recently been killed just like Michelle, but the police "were keeping it quiet." Realizing that a lack of clear information has a tendency to breed conspiracy theories, authorities tried their best to rebut these claims.

Meanwhile, investigators had zeroed in on a convicted rapist, who had attacked a Cedar Rapids woman with a knife. The suspect always denied killing Michelle Martinko, though, and he was eventually cleared by DNA evidence before passing away from cancer in 2012.

Another person of interest was an ex-boyfriend named Andy Seidel. Andy and Michelle had met a couple of years ago when they were both high school sophomores. Michelle's friend Gail Dawson would later recall how she and Michelle first met Andy at a local roller-skating rink. Andy, who was 16 and a newly licensed driver, impressed Michelle with the "flashy sports car" that he drove, and the two would go on to date for two years before they broke up.

According to those who knew them, it was not a good breakup. Andy longed for Michelle to take him back, but Michelle, now focused on her senior year of high school and preparations for college, was not interested in rekindling their old romance. Friends and family would later suggest that Andy had been somewhat stalking his ex-girlfriend, trying to keep track of "her every move"—and some went further and insinuated that Michelle's jilted ex-boyfriend had killed her out of pure bitterness and malice. Further adding to the shroud of suspicion surrounding Andy Seidel was the fact that he had actually been at the Westdale Mall on the very day that Michelle died. But as police would discover, he had gone home before Michelle even got there, and he had a solid alibi as to where he was later that night when she was killed.

Police also looked into another guy that Michelle had dated—a former high school classmate named Mike Wyrick. Mike had already graduated and was attending college some 100 miles away, but this didn't keep him completely off the police radar. Mike would later recall that the cops really grilled him about his previous relationship with Michelle. In one interrogation session, they even showed him grisly crime scene photos to see his reaction. Such treatment was tantamount to torture for Mike, who cared deeply about Michelle, but he tried to take it in stride and help the police as much as he could. He was so cooperative, in fact, that they eventually decided that he was very unlikely to be the killer.

That meant they were fresh out of suspects, though, and as the years wore on without any definitive leads, the case became increasingly cold. In their desperation for results, detectives tried a wide variety of techniques to jump-start the investigation. They experimented with using hypnosis on witnesses who'd been at the Westdale Mall that night, to see if they could remember more details that way. At one point they even employed a psychic. But none of it was any use, and in the end, it wasn't clairvoyance that would break this case open, but rather pure crime scene forensics.

In the mid-2000s, a detective newly assigned to the cold case stumbled upon something that had been overlooked for decades: a blood sample that had been recovered from the gearshift on Michelle's car. This blood did not belong to Michelle, and modern DNA analysis showed that it belonged to an unknown male.

What was this man's blood doing in Michelle's car? Was it from her assailant? Did he get cut and bleed while he was attacking Michelle?

Investigators wanted answers to those questions, so they built up a DNA profile based on the blood specimen and scoured their database of registered offenders for a match. They didn't find one—but several years later, a new technique came to prominence.

Instead of just looking into criminal DNA databases, investigators now also look at familial DNA database collections. We've all seen those TV commercials for companies like ancestry.com that allow folks to submit their DNA in order to trace their family tree. Well, these databases have grown considerably in recent years, and they have become a treasure trove for investigators by way of something called genetic genealogy. This allows police to track down not the perpetrator, but relatives of the perpetrator. Even distant cousins of a person who's left DNA at a crime scene can be identified through this technique.

And it was in fact a second cousin of their eventual suspect that investigators working the Michelle Martinko case first identified. They were then able to trace back to this cousin's great, great grandparents, and then work their way back down to the immediate family of the suspect himself. It was a time-consuming process, but it eventually narrowed down the blood from the gearshift to three brothers.

Police then carefully tracked all three men and covertly collected additional DNA samples from them in order to establish a link. When they picked up a discarded plastic straw that had been used by Jerry Lynn Burns and sent it in for testing, sure enough—the DNA on the straw and the DNA from the bloody gearshift were a match. Burns was arrested on December 19, 2018, and another DNA sample taken then also proved to be a match to the blood at the crime scene.

Burns, though, steadfastly proclaimed his innocence. And at his trial, he even put forth a plausible reason why his blood was present on the gearshift of Michelle's car. Burns had been working as a mechanic at the local Buick dealership at the time—

and the dealership's records showed that Michelle had indeed taken her car in for repairs. Burns argued that he might have nicked his hand while working on the car, then deposited some blood on the gearshift when he drove it out of the garage. The presence of his DNA was just one big coincidence. Burns also maintained that he did not even know Michelle and had no reason to kill her. And he reminded jurors that he was a young family man at the time, with a wife and kids. How unlikely it would be for such a man to stab a young girl to death for no apparent reason?

Burns' defense highlights the intriguing fact that the presence of someone's DNA at a crime scene isn't always proof of guilt—but in the Michelle Martinko case, the jury thought that it was. After a brief deliberation, they came back with a guilty verdict.

The Conviction

Jerry Lynn Burns stood trial for the murder of Michelle Martinko in early 2020 and was found guilty on February 24th. On August 7th, he was handed a life sentence. Burns, however, still maintains his innocence.

Chris Steiner
At the Mercy
of The Bone Crusher

Who: Chris Steiner
Where: Baraboo, Wisconsin
When: July 1994
Suspects: Joe Clark
Conviction: 1997

Background Information

Chris Steiner was a typical 14-year-old Wisconsin boy who enjoyed riding his bike and hanging out with his friends. But in the summer of 1994, his life took a strange and tragic detour. For on the eve of the Fourth of July, he was snatched right out of his home and subjected to horrendous abuse.

Chris Steiner's parents woke up on the morning of Independence Day to find their son missing. There were obvious signs of a break-in. A window screen had been cut open and muddy footprints had been tracked into their home. Someone had clearly come into their home in the middle of the night and taken their son. The panicked Steiners alerted police, and a search was conducted in a desperate effort to find the boy. He was indeed found about six days later—but at that point, he was no longer among the living. His corpse was discovered caught on a tree, floating in the Wisconsin River.

The Investigation

As suspicious as Chris's death might sound, investigators actually deemed it to be accidental after an autopsy showed that he had drowned. Ignoring the possibility that he had been forced under the water by someone else, they simply assumed that he had snuck out of his house in the middle of the night and fallen into the river. And that's where the case might have remained forever—if another local boy hadn't very nearly ended up suffering the same fate a little over a year later.

In July of 1995, little Thad Phillips was taken from his home after falling asleep on the couch in his parent's living room. Thad would later recall opening his eyes to find himself being carried by a stranger, who hoisted him up in the air and took him right out the front door. In his disoriented state, he initially thought it was one of his parents. After the intruder set him down outside, however, and Thad got a good look at him, he realized that it wasn't his mom and dad.

Still, the trusting boy decided that he must somehow know this person. Perhaps it was a family friend. For a small, sleepy child struggling to make sense of the situation, that seemed like a possibility. And besides, the young man who had carried him out the door seemed friendly enough—even downright enthusiastic. So, when he challenged the boy to a footrace, Thad started running. The next thing he knew, he was far from home and unsure how to get back. Just like Hansel and Gretel in the enchanted forest, he realized that he was now hopelessly lost. But while it may sound like a fairy tale, this is actually what happened.

Unable to find his way home on his own, Thad felt he had no choice but to continue following the stranger, who then led him all the way to his house. His host invited him in and introduced himself as Joe. He then herded the boy up into an upstairs room where he said he had some "cool model cars" he wanted to show him. But rather than show off his Hot Wheels collection, Joe shut the door behind him and turned on his guest. That's when things got really ugly.

Joe picked the boy up, tossed him onto the bed, and jumped on top of him. Then he grabbed Thad's foot, and despite the child's cries, mercilessly twisted it until the bones of his ankle broke with a sickening snap. As much pain as Thad was in, he managed to summon the strength to break free from his attacker. He fell off the bed and crawled/limped his way out of the room, struggling all the way down the stairs before Joe reached him, picked him up, and tossed him onto a nearby couch. His brutal captor then grabbed his injured foot and yanked his entire leg up over his head, until his thigh bone gave out and broke in half.

Bizarrely, after inflicting this bone-breaking trauma on the child, Joe then amused himself by playing doctor. Joe, who later admitted to having a fascination with bones and setting casts, actually dressed Thad's broken leg and foot with "socks and Ace bandages." This sadistic "doctor" then carefully carried his patient back to the upstairs bedroom and laid him in bed. Joe apparently figured that his victim was as good as immobilized at this point, and he took the opportunity to leave and meet up with his girlfriend.

While he was out, with a tremendous struggle, Thad overcame the pain to get himself out of the bed and on down the stairs. He managed to get as far as the kitchen before Joe came back with his girlfriend. Thad heard them come in and lay down as stiff as a board in the kitchen while they sat on the couch. Unable to get away, Thad stayed in this sorry state for quite some time.

When Joe's girlfriend finally left, Joe made his way into the kitchen and discovered Thad lying on the floor. Joe was shocked that the kid could have dragged himself that far in such a condition, but his shock soon gave way to rage as he grabbed the boy up and took him upstairs for more abuse. He beat him and openly threatened to take his life. Thad was now beginning to think that this was Joe's intention all along—and that it would be just a matter of time before Joe made good on the threat.

The next time Joe left was on July 30th. This time he took the extra precaution of locking Thad up in a bedroom closet. His situation must have seemed hopeless, but once he was sure that Joe was gone, Thad once again put his determination to work.

This time the little boy grabbed an old guitar that was locked in the closet with him. With a feat of strength that seemed to be in advance of his years, he used it to break down the door. Thad was not able to walk, but he could drag himself. And that's what he did. With his little hands as his only means of locomotion, he dragged himself out of that room, on down the stairs, and straight to the kitchen.

The last time he was there, he had noticed a telephone, and this time he made his way right to it. Picking up the receiver, he dialed 911. The emergency dispatcher was astonished at his story. It was almost too painful to listen to—and almost too hard to believe. Fortunately, they did believe him, and after tracing his location, they immediately sent the police to rescue him.

At this point, Thad had been missing for a full 43 hours. The damage he sustained during this period would last him for a lifetime. To this very day, he walks with a limp due to the abuse that he suffered through. His quick thinking, however, led to the arrest of 17-year-old Joe Clark.

The charges Clark faced for the kidnapping and battery of Thad Phillips were bad enough, but he was soon suspected of the murder of Chris Stein as well. Thad himself testified that Clark had told him that he had victimized others and that one of those victims was a boy named Chris. And when police searched Clark's home, they were shocked to find, written on a sheet of paper in a notebook, an elaborate listing of other local boys he wanted to brutalize.

Nevertheless, Clark continued to profess his innocence. Even though Thad had been found with broken legs in his own home, he insisted that he didn't have any knowledge of how he got there. Even stranger was the fact that Clark's mother swore she hadn't noticed the brutality either. How could she not notice what was happening in her own home? The only explanation that she offered was that she was a "sound sleeper."

Denials aside, the evidence against Joe Clark was more than strong enough for an autopsy on Chris Steiner's body to be ordered. This revealed that Chris's legs had been broken just like Thad's, and this changed everything. Chris hadn't accidentally drowned; Clark had broken his legs before throwing him into the river so that he would be unable to swim.

The Conviction

Joe Clark was tried for Chris Stein's murder in 1997 and ultimately found guilty. His conviction solved this cold case and helped close an altogether disturbing chapter in the annals of criminal history.

Hilda Murrell
Cold Case Solved?

Who: Hilda Murrell
Where: Shropshire, England
When: January 1984
Suspects: Andrew George
Conviction: 2003

Background Information

Hilda Murrell, born in 1906, was a pleasant and widely admired elderly lady at the time of her death in 1984. This accomplished woman from an esteemed family graduated from Britain's University of Cambridge in 1927. Ten years later she took over her family's floral business in Shropshire, Edwin Murrell Nurseryman & Seed Merchant, when her father's health began to decline. The business specialized in rose gardens and was known all over England for its produce.

Upon her retirement in the 1970s, Hilda became an avid environmentalist, which in turn led her to protest against Britain's development of nuclear energy. She immersed herself in British liberalism and environmental issues throughout that decade, and by the early 1980s, she had made quite a name for herself. When the Falklands War broke out in 1982, she sparked the ire of the British government by holding large gatherings at her estate which amounted to strategy sessions for the protest movement. The following year, with Britain set to increase its nuclear arsenal, she sponsored the local Nuclear Freeze campaign. Later that same year, Hilda Murrell composed a well-thought-out essay on the state of nuclear energy, which she called "An Ordinary Citizen's View of Radioactive Waste Management."

Hilda Murrell was scheduled to make a public appearance to voice her critiques of nuclear energy, but shortly before the event was to take place, she was assaulted, robbed, kidnapped, and murdered. She was held for a short time before her body was discarded in a field.

Although at first glance the killing seemed to be the work of a particularly murderous burglar, due to the high-profile nature of Murrell's activism, conspiracy theories began to circulate that perhaps there was more to her death than it appeared. Some even speculated that it was a hit carried out by MI5 (the British secret police) to silence a known opposition leader.

The Investigation

Ignoring the conspiracy theories, investigators took the most obvious route and proceeded on the assumption that Hilda Murrell had fallen prey to a random burglar. They soon zeroed in on was a 16-year-old who had done some work on the estate— Andrew George. George had been arrested for burglary once before, but the charges had been dropped. And other than that, there was nothing to suggest that he might have been involved in Hilda's death. With insufficient evidence to arrest George and no other suspects in sight, they were forced to let the case grow cold.

It was only in 2003 that advances in DNA forensics enabled investigators to retrieve George's DNA from Hilda's underwear. Yes, sadly enough, Hilda had suffered through a sexual assault before she was killed—and the semen the violation left behind pointed the finger back at Andrew George.

The Conviction

With the new DNA evidence in hand, Andrew George was arrested, tried, and in 2005, convicted of Hilda Murrell's murder. He was given a life sentence, which required him to serve a minimum of 15 years before any possibility of parole.

Lynette White
Finding Her Bloody Valentine Killer

Who: Lynette White
Where: Cardiff, Wales (United Kingdom)
When: February 1988
Suspects: Jeffrey Gafoor
Conviction: 2003

Background Information

Lynette White was a young woman whose life had taken a wrong turn. She grew up in Britain's bustling South Wales and had begun to run with a bad crowd. Drinking, drugs, and sex had become her main pastimes. She was selling her body for a living when her life came to an end on the dark Valentine's Day morning of 1988.

During the wee hours of February 14, 1988, Lynette picked up a prospective John and took him back to her apartment. This run-down joint on top of a storefront was in perpetual darkness since the utilities had been cut due to unpaid bills—but the darkness suited Lynette's type of business just fine. Lynette knew the routine. She would get on her shabby mattress, her John would have his way with her, and then she would get paid. Routine, nothing more and nothing less.

But on this particular night, something went wrong. It would later be learned from the Johns' own testimony that the two got into a fight overpayment. The man wasn't happy with the services Lynette had provided him and suddenly demanded a refund. Lynette, however, steadfastly refused to give back the money she had just earned. When John realized that the renegotiation was going nowhere, he reached for a knife and stabbed Lynette multiple times before cutting her throat. She never had a chance.

The Investigation

A few hours later, Lynette White's bloody corpse was discovered and reported to the police. The cops were shocked when they saw what had become of her. Yes, she was a prostitute who regularly worked the wrong side of the tracks. And yes, prostitutes do regularly meet with foul play by the men they sleep with. But the sheer brutality of this assault was shocking even to veteran detectives. Lynette had over 50 stab wounds on her body, and her breasts were also mutilated in such a horrific fashion that it seemed clear that the perpetrator had a real sadistic streak.

South Wales could be a rough place, but who would do something like this? Initially, police zeroed in on Lynette's pimp, Stephen Miller. Pimps, after all, are well known for beating and threatening their girls—and sometimes they kill one *pour encourager les autres*. As it turned out, however, Miller had a pretty solid alibi; he'd been out at local pool hall when Lynette was killed, and he had several witnesses willing to testify to this.

Nevertheless, police still insisted on charging Miller with the murder. It seems that they made a deliberate decision to pin it on him despite the evidence of his innocence. And while it's true that Stephen Miller was not exactly an upstanding citizen, this was a shocking abuse of power—it's flat-out illegal for police to knowingly charge someone for a crime they didn't commit. Yet this is apparently what happened.

Miller, who had some kind of "mental difficulty", was not able to defend himself very well. He didn't seem to grasp that his alibi of shooting pool with friends should have been enough to clear him. On the contrary, after being interrogated for several hours on end, he cracked under the pressure and ended up confessing. Having gotten that far, the police then put the squeeze on Miller so hard that he named some associates of his—Ronnie Actie, John Actie, Yusuf Abdullahi, and Tony Paris—as his accomplices in the killing. This led to all five of these men being charged for a crime they had nothing to do with.

How do we know this? Because the true killer eventually did come forward.

The Conviction

In what has been described as Britain's "greatest miscarriage of justice" in modern memory, five men were railroaded for a crime they did not commit. Stephen Miller, Yusuf Abdullahi, and Tony Paris were found guilty, while Ronnie and John Actie were acquitted. The police had focused more on the personal backgrounds and history of these men rather than the facts of what actually happened to Lynette White—but their malfeasance would soon come to light.

After Miller, Abdullahi, and Paris were put behind bars, a small grassroots campaign calling for their release was organized. This push quickly gained steam as members of the community became convinced that these men—known collectively as "the Cardiff Three"—were innocent. Their relentless efforts eventually led to the release of all three in December of 1992. It was a real shame that these men had to spend time behind bars for a crime they did not commit—and even worse, while police were focused on the wrong people, Lynette's real killer was still on the loose.

After all of the drama surrounding the wrongful convictions, it seemed that Lynette's case had gone completely cold. But then, in 1998, a new discovery was made. Small drops of blood that had been overlooked before were discovered on a package of cigarettes that had been found at the crime scene. This blood was sent to a lab for DNA testing, and police then sifted through their database to see if they could find a match. The closest match they found was a bit puzzling since it came from a lad who'd been all of four years old at the time of the killing.

Apparently, even the crooked cops of Cardiff didn't feel up to standing in front of a jury and claiming that a 4-year-old had been out stabbing hookers at three in the morning. So they started looking at the boy's relatives and soon focused their attention on one Jeffrey Gafoor. Gafoor worked as a security guard and had a minimal criminal history—just one infraction for a "minor assault."

But when his DNA proved to be a match for the DNA found at the scene of Lynette's slaying, they began to suspect that he was capable of much more than minor assault.

During questioning, Gafoor admitted that he had had sex with Lynette White and suggested that his semen might have been found on her for this reason. That was certainly plausible; the only problem, of course, was that it wasn't Gafoor's semen that had been found—it was his blood. That was a little harder to explain away, and so police took a fresh DNA sample and put Gafoor under regular surveillance.

Ironically, that ended up saving his life. Knowing that the jig was up, Gafoor tried to end it all by overdosing on acetaminophen (the active ingredient in Tylenol). Police, who'd been watching his every move, then burst into his residence and took him to get medical treatment.

If they hadn't, Jeffrey Gafoor most likely would have taken the tale of what actually happened to Lynette White with him to his grave. But he recovered, and after his near-death experience, he abandoned his excuses, confessed to all that he had done, and pled guilty as charged. In 2003, he was handed a life sentence.

Tina Faelz
Killed by a Classmate

Who: Tina Faelz
Where: Pleasanton, California
When: April 1984
Suspects: Steven Carlson
Conviction: 2014

Background Information

The girl remembered as Tina Faelz began life as Tina Penix. She was born to Ron and Shirley Penix on April 27, 1969. Ron was a native of Washington State who had met Shirley while he was drifting around San Francisco, California, with some friends in the late 1960s. It was love at first sight, and Ron promptly called up his folks back home and told them that he would be back up to see them soon—with the new love of his life in tow.

When they reached Washington, they decided to settle down and stay. They married in 1968, and Baby Tina was born the following year. But Ron hadn't quite given up his wild ways, and his penchant for drinking and carousing led Shirley to take Tina back to California on her own. Ron, who apparently fell out of love as quickly as he fell into it, didn't make much of an effort to contact his wife or daughter after that.

Back in her native California, Shirley moved to Castro Valley, where she became reacquainted with an old high school flame named Steve Faelz. They married in 1973 and purchased a home in Pleasanton, where Tina's half-brother, Steve Jr., was born on November 27, 1975. Despite their six-year age gap, Tina was very close to Steve Jr. They were always running around their neighborhood together, and eventually Tina grew into an athletic girl and played on the soccer team at school.

Shirley worked at the local 7-Eleven convenience store and was a familiar figure to all the neighborhood kids who would come by for snacks, sodas, and a good game of Donkey Kong. Her short, round physique reminded them of the alien from a current Stephen Spielberg blockbuster and earned her the rather unflattering nickname "ET".

Tina was quite popular with her classmates during elementary school, known as a rambunctious prankster. By junior high, though, her peers no longer considered it quite so cool to pull pranks, climb trees, and play ball. Most of them had left such things behind for what they considered to be more "mature" activities, and Tina found it difficult to adapt.

Things got a little complicated in 1982 when Tina's stepdad Steve left the family for another woman. The divorce was bad enough, but to make matters worse, Steve's new wife was none other than the ex-wife of his ex-wife's little brother. Yes, the situation was every bit as convoluted and complicated as that last sentence sounded. Tina, just as she was entering adolescence, had to deal with the bewildering situation of her former stepdad hooking up with her uncle's former wife. This meant that cousins were suddenly siblings, and just about everything to do with family life was jumbled up in complete upheaval. Family reunions were going to be quite complicated from then on, to say the least.

And you can only imagine the schoolyard taunts that Tina must have been subjected to in that close-knit community where everyone knew everyone's business. Her mom was the ET from the 7-Eleven, and her ex-stepdad was married to her former aunt. Such things are simply hard to live down in the pressure cooker we call the public school system, and from this point forward, Tina was frequently bullied by her peers.

She made one good friend, however, in the form of Lisa Celeste, whose mom also worked at the 7-Eleven. Lisa's mother was a single mom, just like Shirley now was, and interestingly enough, just as Tina and Lisa became friends, their mothers became pals as well. After their shifts at the 7-Eleven ended, they would often go hang out together at local bars while their young daughters kept each other company. Many might consider this neglect, but it was simply everyday life for Tina Faelz.

It was in the midst of this instability that Tina began her freshman year at Foothill High School in 1983. By this time, being the regular butt of jokes had made her unbearably shy at school. Nevertheless, she managed to make another new friend, a girl from her neighborhood named Katie Kelly. Katie would later recall just how rough it was for Tina her freshman year. The popular kids would actually throw rocks at her while she waited at the bus stop, and her peers didn't do anything to intervene. On one occasion, another girl who was waiting for the bus even asked, "Can you stand somewhere else so we don't accidentally get hit by a rock?"

By the second half of the school year, in early 1984, the teasing had gotten so bad that Tina gave up on riding the bus and began walking back and forth to school. She soon learned a dangerous shortcut—a tunnel that ran under the freeway. Many kids used this shortcut, but it certainly wasn't a safe environment for a young girl to walk through alone.

When her former stepdad Steve Faelz heard about this, he tried to intervene. Taking Tina to a restaurant to eat some burgers and fries, he asked her why she was walking to school. In what must have been a truly heartbreaking scene, Tina began to cry as she described the abuse that she had suffered from other kids at the bus stop. She insisted that she would rather walk than go through that again. Steve strongly advised her against it, but Tina wouldn't be persuaded. Steve would later come to regret that he wasn't firmer in his insistence that she should take the bus—and after his former stepdaughter turned up dead, he would regret it for the rest of his life.

On April 5, 1984, Tina failed to come home from school. She had been ambushed by her 16-year-old schoolmate Steven Carlson. Carlson got the drop on his 14-year-old prey during her walk and attacked her with a kitchen knife, stabbing her a total of 44 times. Her body was spotted and reported by a truck driver who was driving by—and this trucker's common decency of reporting a crime caused him to become the first suspect in her death. Many in the community jumped to the wrong conclusions and began calling for his arrest. Fortunately, police were able to clear the trucker fairly early on in the investigation. Unfortunately, they didn't have anyone else on their list of suspects.

The Investigation

Who killed Tina was basically anyone's guess. Investigators vacillated between the theory that it was just a random stranger she met along the way and the idea that Tina was purposefully targeted by someone who knew her. At one point, they seriously speculated that it might have been one of her mother's many boyfriends. But without any real leads, this case quickly grew cold.

It wasn't until 2011 that a major break came. Some blood spatter retrieved from Tina's purse all those years ago was tested with modern DNA forensic techniques, and this produced a surprising match to a guy who grew up with Tina—lived in her neighborhood, in fact—Steven Carlson.

It then came to light that Carlson had been a troubled youth with a reputation for harassing girls in the neighborhood. It seems that he may have simply targeted Tina as a crime of opportunity when he caught her walking alone that day. Some of Carlson's friends would later admit that he had joked about being the murderer. They hadn't found the joke funny then, and when Carlson found himself in handcuffs in 2011, even he couldn't see the humor in it anymore.

The Conviction

Steven Carlson was arrested in 2011 on charges of first-degree murder. He immediately denied any involvement in Tina's death, and he maintained his innocence throughout his 2014 trial. However, he was ultimately convicted and handed a sentence of 26 years to life. However, his conviction was later reduced to second-degree murder, in acknowledgment that the crime was most likely not premeditated.

It wasn't until 2020, six years after he was found guilty, that Steven Carlson finally admitted that he had killed Tina Faelz. In letters written from his jail cell, Carlson claimed that he didn't set out to kill her. He stated that he was angry about being picked on at school, and frustrated with his home life, and he took it out on her.

After a particularly bad day, he grabbed a kitchen knife, put it in his pocket, and stormed outside. When he then ran into Tina, he blacked out in a rage and just began stabbing her. According to Carlson, the next thing he knew, he was standing over her bloody body with the knife in hand. It's hard to tell how truthful this convicted killer might be, but if nothing else, at least he did finally come around to admitting his guilt. And none too soon— Steven Carlson will be eligible for parole in 2023.

Bringing Solace to Society

If you ask any veteran investigator what phrase sounds like music to their ears, it would be three simple words—*cold case solved*. For those who have spent decades searching through evidence and interviewing witnesses and potential suspects, the knowledge that they have finally found justice for the long-departed is rewarding indeed.

And not just for themselves, but for society in general. Since we civilized human beings live under a certain set of rules and norms, it helps us to reinforce the very social charter when those who break the rules are brought to justice. It is humanity's sense of law and order that separates us from the wild beasts of the field. Without laws, we would quickly be reduced to incessant tribal warfare in which the strongest (or maybe just the most vicious) bands strive incessantly for domination.

Without a tight social compact to prevent such abuse, there would be no inventions, no progress—it would be everyone for themselves, living in a miserable state of constant violence and trauma. There would have been no landing on the Moon or Mars if we had to spend all of our time guarding against gangs of outlaws. This is why bringing these murderous transgressors to justice is so important. It not only brings solace to the family, but it also brings solace to an entire society that needs to know that its own rules are being respected and followed.

Further Readings

Here are some of the reading and reference materials that helped to make this text possible. Feel free to explore more of the details of some of the cases presented in this book.

Murder in Pleasanton: Tina Faelz and the Search for Justice. Joshua Suchon
This book focuses solely on the murder of Tina Faelz and does a great job in providing the backstory of both the victim and her convicted killer. If you would like to gain a better understanding of the context of Tina's case, this book is a great place to start.

Criminal Cold Cases: Fugitives Finally Brought to Justice. Charlotte Greig
This text contains an anthology of various cold cases that have been solved throughout the years. Mr. Greig's book provides a great overview of several cases.

www.cnn.com
Many of the more recent cases featured in this book have breaking news articles detailing the cases and subsequent convictions. CNN is a good resource to find more information.